in a nutshell

avery ---

BookLeaf Publishing

India | USA | UK

Presentation by *BookLeaf Publishing*

Web: www.bookleafpub.com

E-mail: info@bookleafpub.com

ISBN: 9789360944766

First edition 2024

PREFACE

hello, lovelies!
here you'll find a collection of all different kinds of poems. as my first poetry book, i wanted variety. many of these were written a couple of years ago (between 2022 and 2023), with the exception of a few newer pieces i've thrown in, as my writing style changes rather consistently.

ocean of flowers

i brought, for you
an   o c e a n   of (flowers)

so when i
w   r   a   p
aro-
-und- you
with a sp-
lash-
, water erupts (and)
sorrow feels forgotten

for we are en---
-trapped.
-closed.
-caged.
by the (beauty) of:

(wilted) rose   p e t a l s
si
    n
        k
    i
ng
(to the) bottom

of an

.

.

.

endless   (pit)

things

when we moved, we went
to a house half the size as the one
we lived in before. half of our old things
got thrown away, anyway.
bags, boxes, trashcans full each week
of old papers, objects, things we didn't need.
it almost looked like a hoarder house off of
one of those tv shows.
and now we have a storage unit full
of things we probably don't need:
old books and paintings, stuffed animals,
empty notebooks, faded shirts, other things.
every now and then, i remember, though,
some important things that are in there:
my great grandmother's pink rose china set,
things mum kept from when we were first born.
but everything else will end up
useless, one day. one day when we're all gone,
when we're all dead. i know that sounds dark,
but
i don't mean it as sad; i mean it as true.

c

called a cloud carrier, i often am. for i
carry clouds in my cups of coffee. i put
coconut & cocoa in my cool drinks or i
crush candy canes & drop them in. i
collect cold coins in a charcoal canteen &
combine them with carrots and lettuce. then i
call them my dreams with crowbars. a
cloud collector, i'm often called, for i
carry clouds in my cups of coffee.

nebula

comets circling covers, chasing her eclipse.
intense ripples of pleasure vibrating her spine.
drawing constellations on her bare chest
until her bright pink nebula exploads.

river

take me to the river: where the good
poets go to die swiftly: where Percy Shelly
passed on the eighth of july as storms
collided with his boat. where Virginia Woolf
filled her pockets with handfuls of
rocks then jumped. where Alfonsina Storni
walked into the sea until she drowned.
take me to the river: where i can inhale
the cool water in little breaths and bring
massive splashes to the surface as my
flailing arms wave their last goodbyes
and my feet finally stop kicking. when i'm
done, watch my empty body sink just
below the surface, where it will slowly
be filled with more of that clear liquid death.
come back in forty-two hours and you will
find me surfaced, face down, floating,
finally oblivious and happy.

the day

when will come the day
in which we do not hold up the world
but it holds itself
when the darkest parts of the moon
will lighten at the touch
of an astronauts fingertips

and when will come the day
in which the wind does not cry
out of pity and sorrow, but of relief
because the leaves have fallen
without the feeling of death
overlapping an entire forest of trees

when will come the day
in which the sour tears
of our mothering planet fade away
at the sound of countless cheers
and yells of happy children
who care not what the world thinks

when will come the day
in which society learns to kneel
out of obedience - not pain -
when will come that day
when, i ask of you
when, when, when

dancing on your hand

i'd like to   slip around
   your calloused
      ukulele playing fingers
         and slide down
      your smooth thumb

to   dangle
   from your middle
      and play hopscotch around
         the cracks and crevices
      of your soft palm

to   skip and dance
   around the tips of
      your short nails until
         my body aches from
      the sharp movements

shadow of the moon

the (shadow)
  of   the (moon)   h
                      a
              n
        g
     s
    deep ; low

   it sits ; (drifts) ; in
(distilled   s i l e n c e)

     it (orbits)
       v   e
   o   r

      and

      o   u
   r (earth) n
    a   d
     .

did

i drifted along a flame for you
and called its sparks to the edge
of my fingertips, i traced them and
told the darkness to hush.

and it did.

i forced a goblet unto you and begged
of you to drink that nectar. i put
it to your lips, but you, not thirsty, didn't
want it the same way i craved.

and i did.

i offered you an open door, and you
took it silently; you walked out
with your head practically rolling off
your shoulders. i said goodbye.

and you did.

sometimes

i found you after the marshes of deep mud
and dark water. clouded skies parted.
you were brown-eyed and quick-tongued
wearing an oversized, faded, grey t-shirt
blue jeans, ripped at the knees
worn out red tennis shoes with torn souls
long dirty socks hid your thin ankles.

they hated you, too, this town did.
they condemned you to hell, too
and perhaps that's why i took to you so well;
to those curled lips that formed a nasty smile
with teeth that hadn't been brushed for days.
but now, when you crawl back into my mind,
a drink helps, sometimes. sometimes.

you should've been born in the 80's.
you'd have fit in better there, with your puffy
black hair, sticking straight up in the mornings,
slicked back when you went to meetings.
your brown skin glittered in moonlight.
you were not troubled by bullets or grenades,
in fact, you preferred them to the dust.

and no matter how i tried, reaching you

was like touching the eye of a hurricane:
angry winds surrounded you. your inside
was nothing but red, red, red, red.
you were infectious.
but now, when my dark dreams come,
a drink helps, sometimes. sometimes.

breath

when you take
my breath
away from me
you must give it back
otherwise
i will not be able
to live
without you

and when you steal
my prosperity
and leave me
with sorrow
you must not
come back begging
otherwise
i might let you

adrenaline junkie

a princess in black heels, cackling a
hyena laugh. rocking out to nirvana
in her underwear, alone, while under
other covers are secret lovers
wanting, needing the rush

a princess with a dirt bike, reving up
the engine, jamming with pearl, dancing in
an oversized hoodie and not wearing
pants. talking to strangers about
sex, even though she's a virgin

a princess wearing a pink collar. it's
tight around her neck ~ her eyes fixated
on the prize of a million years and a
thousand lives. dusting off reflections
of a kiss from a past life

a princess holding a blender, shredding
chicken sideways. fixing herself with videos
of my chemical romance. imagining a world
where her dreamer exists, even though
she knows that it doesn't

wasn't

there once was a baby
holding up the world with puppet strings
tied to the nicer things of life
such as butter knives and petals
sharp bells from the churches
drifting in lilac and rose and violet fields
but a religious person, he usually wasn't

there once was a boy
hallowed from the inside of his soul, out
with hunched shoulders and long legs
watching pale sunrises made of peach
cobbler and honey, soaked in marble
formed with mountains of money
but a greedy person, he usually wasn't

there once was a man
with a rocky, ruby, red heart in his chest
and a sickness carressing his bones
along with sulking thoughts of dewdrops
and a blow to his blue eyes when he looked
up, so he watched the stone ground
but a gifted person, he usually wasn't

there once was an elder

with white hair atop his head
and a grave at the end of his bed, tears
sliding from the creases in his sockets
after being soaked in wisdom and power
forged from winter chills and grey gunpowder
cause he was constantly told, what he usually
wasn't

the wrong perfection

you've a spearmint flavored mouth,
smoke blowing from the joint
you rolled with toffee colored fingers.

you've smooth skin covered by a cobalt
suit, a glass of red wine in your hand
as we admire a rusting sunset.

you've almond eyes, opened wide
with pepper flakes on the lids
indigo irises, dilated blackberry centers.

you've ultraviolet sunshine in your touch
when you slide in and ask me "champagne?"
but i'm more of a whiskey type of gal.

the thing

I
in the smaller pines
surrounded by nature
growing smaller and
more petite.

II
when shadows are dripping
and faith becomes
~ reality ~
no longer in the pit.

III
when a point is not
a needle, but a long hole
and you end up
living through it twice.

IV
what does it mean,
or even matter,
if the wolves
come out for dinner tonight?

V

in the midst of challenge!
that's where it is most
commonly found. oh,
what is it?

VI
in two minds
at the same time
watching white birds fly
around, dropping feathers.

VII
questioning looks
coming from the animals
that are sitting in
the rain.

VIII
rebellions for wildlife;
signs shouting to "save" it,
even when it was here
first.

IX
ashes come from
the paradise you praised
because it was destroyed
by your selfishness.

X
and now i must
ask you this -
out of curiosity -
what is it?

[i've seen books destroyed.]

i've seen books destroyed.
i've watched individual pages
burn to ash and dust
in the hands of an arsonist
above a red lighter and a yellow flame.
i've watched paperback covers
breathe in water
and i've watched them die
as they sunk to the bottom.

i've watched e-books get
replaced by online pool and poker
and ads for false money making apps.
i've watched school textbooks get
replaced by computers.
while outside, the playground
grows moss on its swings and
tangling vines on its slides.

but their words, their messages
lingered in the back of my brain.
they drifted around, danced, rearranged,
formed new sentences, new ideas;
and eventually my light bulb lit up,
(even if eventually my light bulb will shatter)
because the thoughts, oh, the thoughts,
those stayed.

syrah

i.
i have studied all of the labels
and found merlot, pinot noir, malbec.
but you, syrah, are my favorite.
with your violet eyes
and darkened full body drenched
in a deep red from head to feet.

ii.
it was not easy to catch you, syrah;
you weren't here as oft as the rest.
but my appetite only grew,
it only widened,
as i inhaled your scent
of cocoa and fermented blackberry.

iii.
i caught up with you, syrah,
just outside of the bar, wearing
little more than enough to cover
cleavage and you left
with me. at home, you
covered me with your flavor.

iv.

you disappeared early
the next morning, syrah, before i woke.
you left behind a few strings
of your strawberry blonde curls
over my velvet pillows
and my now-stained satin sheets.

v.
i will not soon forget you, syrah,
nor the way your maroon nails
traced down my back.
you left an aftertaste
of ground black pepper and
spice on my sore tongue.

the poet's cry

doest thou believe in unoriginality?
yes, thee cries, yes!
for even a weeping soul is a cliché
and even he who quoteth
the olden poet is a liar.

i love tears

and the sky wept
the night you left,
because you were no longer
there to dry its eyes.

the sky yelled at the earth
and the ground took it
all in, the same way
the paper takes in ink.

now, when i think of you,
i think of the rain,
and the tears of the
atmosphere above.

(the same tears that:
        watered the flowers
        turned the yellow leaves sour
        and brought the grass to its knees.)

but i loved the tears
that came alongside you
because they gave me
a better reason to breathe.

late night talks

i speak to the moon sometimes, late at night
after everyone's asleep, their eyes shut tight
we whisper and laugh and talk of good times
she helps me write some of tomorrow's rhymes

i speak of the world and things i haven't seen
she speaks of the beauty in our blue and green
i speak of the yearning i feel for her earth
she speaks of the galaxies that are at birth

but even the moon has other things to do
so sometimes she has to go away too
and when she does, i'm left in the dark
wondering and wondering about our old spark

but when i sit alone in times like these
the stars pop out slowly with perfect ease
so i suppose there is always light to be shed
even in the darkest of times in one's head

i write (poetry)

i write (poetry)
because i'm a (poet)
with a bit of a
c   o   k   d
r   o   e
(mind)

i write (poetry)
because i adore
words that d
       a
          n
      g
  l
    e
like (whispering) vines

i write (poetry)
because without it
(the world)
wouldn't feel the
same (b e a u t y)
that it does when it (hears)

a poet's

(c
r
y)